written by
Daphne McMenemy

illustrated by
Alexandria Masse

Gracie the Maker

BEAN BOOKS

This book belongs to

_____

To my mom,
for filling up my box of craft supplies every
weekend my entire childhood.
I am a maker.

To my dad,
who never did anything conventionally.
I am an innovator.

To my brother,
who held my hand every step of the way,
turning every challenge into a chance.
I am brave because of you.

It was Monday morning and it was time for school.

" C'mon Mom! Let's go! "

Gracie said excitedly as she hurried out the door. Gracie couldn't wait to get to school today. Ms. Wilde said today was the day a new classmate was arriving.

Gracie got to school and ran to her classroom. She sat in her usual spot on the carpet with Patrick and Riley. She looked around the room but didn't see any new faces.

That's when Ms. Wilde walked in. Standing next to her was a little girl Gracie didn't recognize.

"Good morning everyone! I'd like you to meet our new classmate, Edie."

The little girl didn't say anything. She just smiled and quietly waved at the class.

"Edie, why don't you hang up your backpack and sit right over there."

Gracie smiled and made room for Edie right beside her.

Gracie	Edie

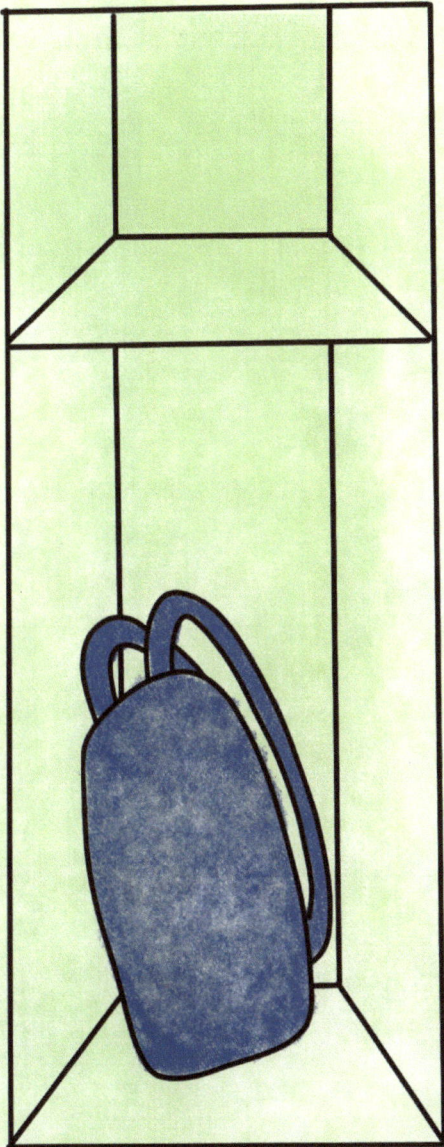

Edie hung up her backpack in the cubby next to Gracie's. Gracie noticed her backpack had robots on it. That's when she knew they were going to be **best friends!**

Edie did as Ms. Wilde asked and sat down next to Gracie.

Gracie turned and whispered, "Hi! I'm Gracie!"

Edie smiled and whispered back, "Hi!"

"I like your backpack!" Gracie said. "Thanks", Edie smiled.

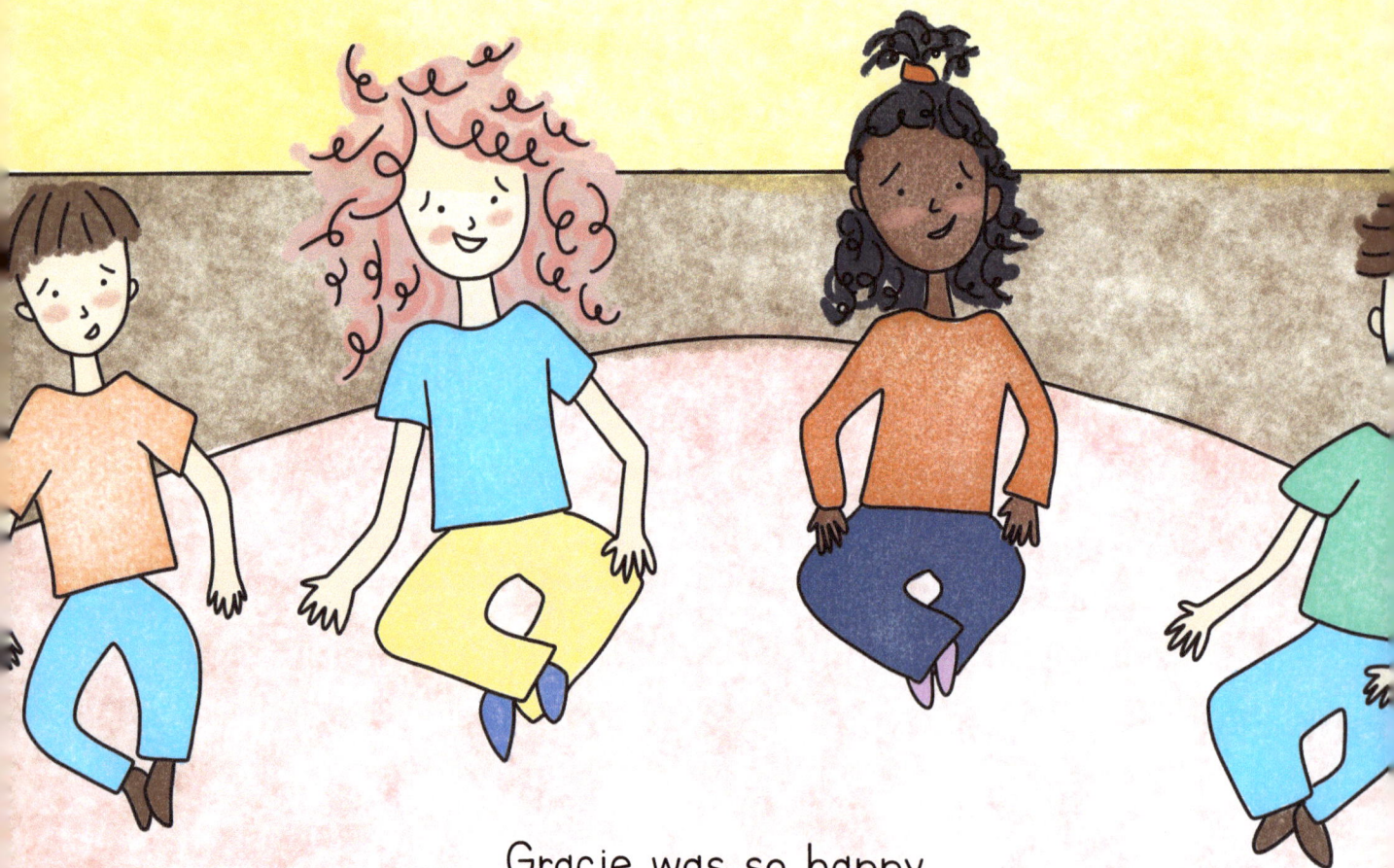

Gracie was so happy.
She **loved** making new friends.

Gracie was excited to show Edie around the classroom. She couldn't wait to show her GoBot, the blocks and dinosaur baskets. But what Gracie was most excited for was introducing Edie to their class pet.

"What's its name?" Edie asked as she walked up to the tortoise.

" **That's Turbo!** " Gracie answered.

"But don't get too close to his tank."

"Why not?" Edie asked.

"He's a baby. He's afraid of us. He'll hide if we get too close." Gracie explained.

And sure enough, as soon as Edie got close to the tank, Turbo hurried into his log and tucked his little head into his shell.

Edie watched Turbo closely. She watched as he poked his head **in** and **out** of his shell to look around. She wondered why he was so frightened.

As soon as Turbo saw Edie peering into his tank, he tucked his head right back in.

Edie noticed that Turbo's food dish was so full
and asked Gracie why.

"Turbo doesn't like when we put our hand in his tank to fill up his dish. He hides in his shell until we leave."

Gracie and Edie wanted to help Turbo. Mrs. Wilde suggested they brainstorm ideas and come up with a plan. She handed them a clipboard, some paper and pencils.

They knew they had to figure out a way to feed Turbo without getting too close to his tank.

"But how will we get his food in there?" Gracie asked.

"We're going to have to make some kind of invention to get his food into his dish from the outside of the tank." Edie said.

They both stared at the tank and wondered what they were going to create. Suddenly, they had an idea!

"A slide!"

they both said at the same time.

The girls got to work right away. They started by sketching out their invention. They were going to make a slide that started at the top of the tank and stopped right in Turbo's dish. A small cup filled with food would sit at the top of the slide.

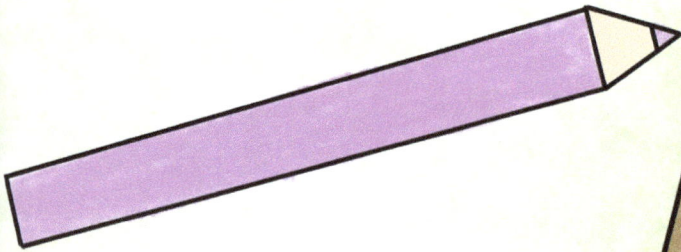

"Hmm...how can we tip the cup without getting too close to Turbo?" Gracie wondered out loud.

Edie looked around the room and noticed GoBot sitting on the shelf. "I have the perfect idea!" she said, "But first, let's make a list of supplies!"

Gracie and Edie wandered the classroom gathering all the materials they needed.

As they collected their supplies, they checked
each item off their list.

The girls sat and looked at their invention sketch. Edie picked up GoBot and a ball and shared her idea with Gracie. "If Turbo doesn't like when we get close to his tank, we can use GoBot instead. We can code GoBot to knock the cup over by tossing the ball at the cup!"

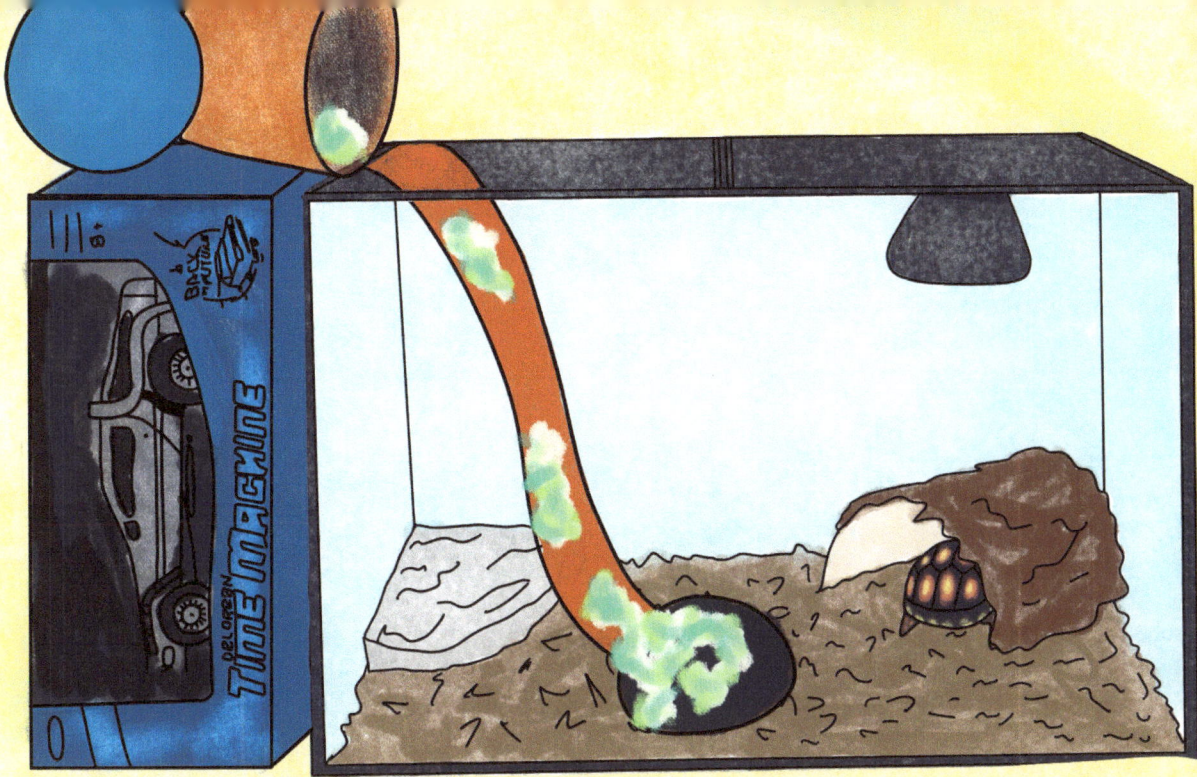

Gracie added, "When the ball hits the cup, it will tip over and the food will slide right into Turbo's bowl! Edie, that's a **great idea!**"

Gracie got to work building the slide.

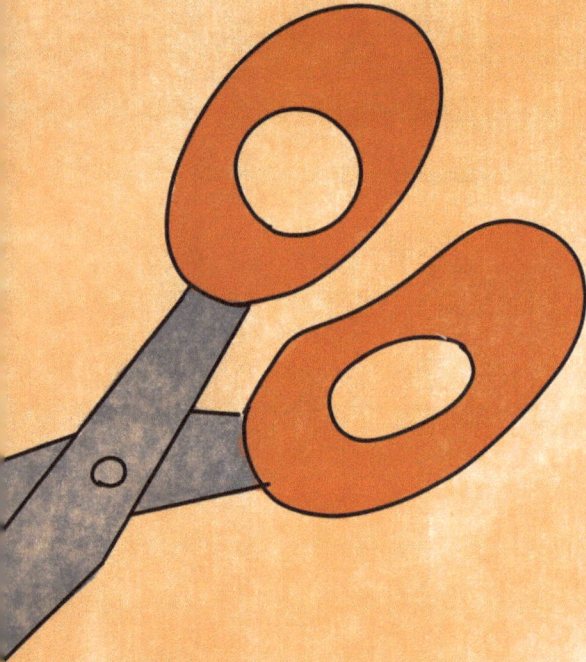

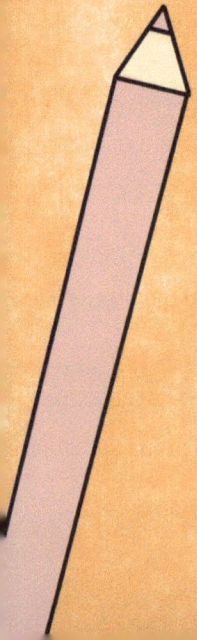

Edie got to work building the code.

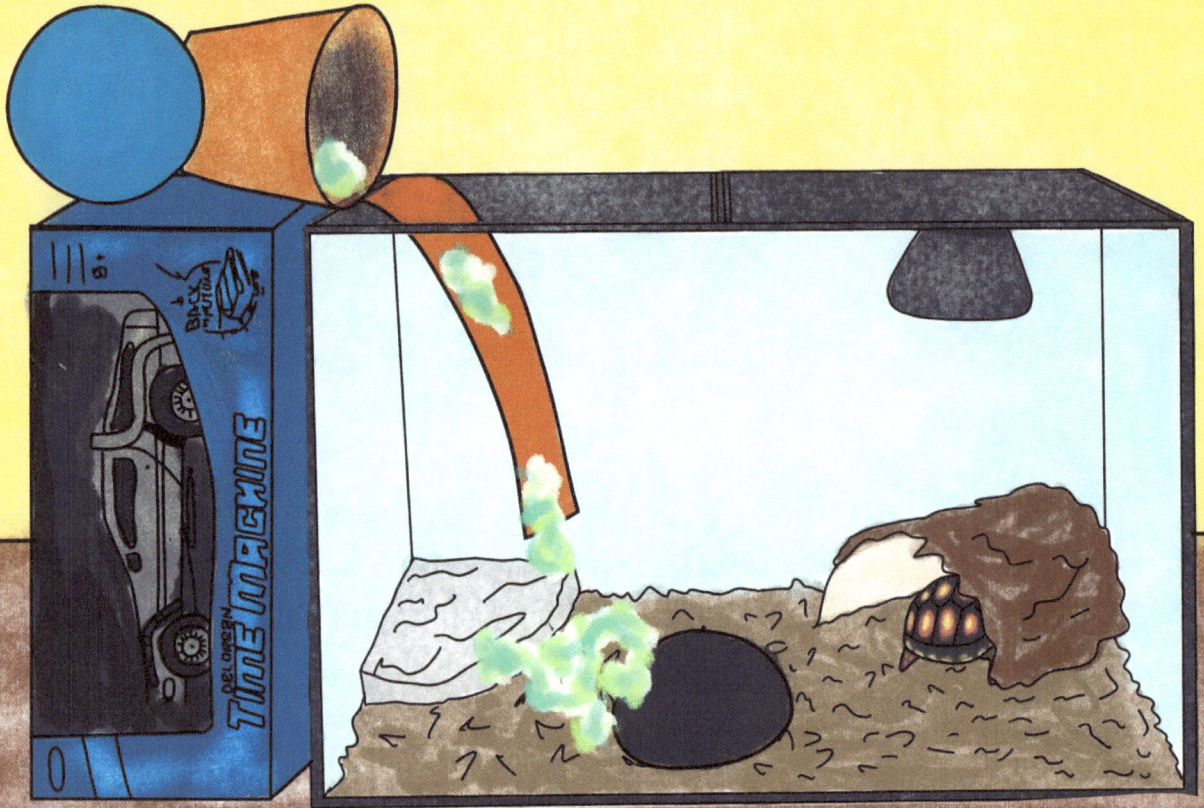

As they built their invention, they tested and
retested. First Gracie's slide was too short.
Then the cup kept tipping over and spilling
food everywhere.

Edie's first code sent GoBot backwards instead of forward. Then GoBot tossed the ball **at Ms. Wilde** instead of Turbo's tank!

The girls spent the day building and rebuilding, testing and retesting. The slide was finally the perfect fit for Turbo's tank. The cup sat perfectly balanced at the top. Together, Gracie and Edie fixed all of the bugs in GoBot's code. They were ready for the final test!

Gracie set GoBot up with the ball. Edie filled
the little cup with food. Turbo poked his head
out of his shell.

There was only one thing left to do.

GO!

GoBot drove straight to Turbo's tank. The robot lit up green, beeped twice, and the little robot arm launched the ball right at the cup! The cup tipped over sending tortoise food down the slide right into Turbo's dish! The little tortoise watched in **amazement!**

Gracie and Edie were so happy. Their invention worked!

Ms. Wilde was so proud. The girls had worked so hard. They never gave up when things didn't work as they planned.

And Turbo? Well, he was so full!

The next morning, Gracie jumped out of bed.
She couldn't wait to get to school!

" **I wonder what
we're going to
invent today.** "

Daphne McMenemy is a Canadian educator, author, speaker, and recipient of the Canadian Prime Minister's Award for Teaching Excellence for her work with coding, robotics, and STEM integration. Her children's book series, Gracie, draws from her classroom experiences of two decades, where she has empowered children to explore learning through innovative STEM approaches. Daphne's classroom expertise empowers hesitant learners, fostering confidence and active engagement. Committed to building relationships and inspiring students through creativity, she is an international speaker and continues make great impact in classrooms across the continent.

Learn more about Daphne at www.daphnemcmenemy.com.

Learn more about Gracie at www.discovergracie.com.

First published in Canada in 2020.
This edition published by Bean Books in 2025.

The Future Belongs
to the Innovators

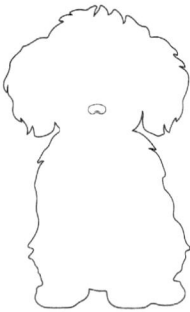

www.ingramcontent.com/pod-product-compliance
Lightning Source LLC
Chambersburg PA
CBHW061053090426
42740CB00003B/135